Math in
the Kitchen

By William Amato

Children's Press®
A Division of Scholastic Inc.
New York / Toronto / London / Auckland / Sydney
Mexico City / New Delhi / Hong Kong
Danbury, Connecticut

Photo Credits: Cover and all photos by Maura Boruchow
Contributing Editor: Jennifer Silate
Book Design: Laura Stein

Library of Congress Cataloging-in-Publication Data

Amato, William.
   Math in the kitchen / by William Amato.
    p. cm. -- (Math in my world)
   Includes index.
   Summary: Simple text and illustrations explain how math is used in the kitchen while baking brownies.
   ISBN 0-516-23939-2 (lib. bdg.) -- ISBN 0-516-23598-2 (pbk.)
   1. Mathematics--Juvenile literature. 2. Cookery--Juvenile literature.
[1. Mathematics. 2. Cookery.] I. Title.
   QA40.5 .A53 2002
513--dc21

                                                              2001037109

Contents

We are making brownies for a **bake sale**.

First, we pour the brownie mix into a bowl.

5

Next, we add oil and water.

7

We also need to add two eggs to the **batter**.

There are twelve eggs in the **carton**.

How many eggs will be left?

There are ten eggs left in the carton.

11

I help Mom **stir** everything together.

13

After we finish stirring, Mom and I pour the batter into a pan.

Mom puts the pan into the oven.

The brownies are done!

Mom cuts them into pieces.

How many brownies
are there?

There are twelve brownies.

We are going to have a good bake sale!

New Words

bake sale (**bayk sayl**) when baked goods like brownies and cakes are sold to raise money

batter (**bat**-uhr) a mixture thin enough to pour that becomes solid when cooked

carton (**kart**-n) a box made of cardboard, heavy paper, or plastic

stir (**ster**) to mix things by moving them around with a spoon

To Find Out More

Books
Alice in Pastaland: A Math Adventure
by Alexandra Wright
Charlesbridge Publishing

Pigs in the Pantry: Fun with Math and Cooking
by Amy Axelrod
Simon & Schuster Children's Press

Web Site
Math Whale
http://www.mathwhale.com/
Math Whale uses cartoon sea animals to teach about numbers and math.

Index

About the Author

William Amato is a teacher and writer living in New York City.

Reading Consultants

Kris Flynn, Coordinator, Small School District Literacy, The San Diego County Office of Education

Shelly Forys, Certified Reading Recovery Specialist, W.J. Zahnow Elementary School, Waterloo, IL

Sue McAdams, Former President of the North Texas Reading Council of the IRA, and Early Literacy Consultant, Dallas, TX